# Grow Money II

## A Teenager's Guide to Saving and Investing

D0317445

By
Michael Pellittiere II

**Grow Money II – A Teenager's Guide to Saving and Investing**

Published by

Dakota Associates Incorporated

For information address: www.DakotaAssociates.com

ISBN: 978-0-6151-8343-5

Printed in The United States of America

Dedicated to

# Andrea

My wife and best friend – Still !!

# Special thanks to

My son Mike for proofreading and providing my
focus by being a Teenager

# A note to the adults

Keep in mind that although I wrote this book with today's teenagers in mind, feel free to share this with kids, and adults, of all ages. In my previous book, *GROW MONEY – A Kid's Guide to Saving and Investing*, I targeted middle school age kids. What I found, and frequently was told and/or noticed, was that it actually applied to and was utilized by a wider age range than I had originally anticipated.

As in the "first" *GROW MONEY,* the percentage amounts at times may seem larger than usually seen. This has been done to more clearly illustrate the effect of interest rates when using smaller principal amounts.

# Table of Contents

# T of C (continued)

## Chapter Eight
### Social Security

## Chapter Nine
### The Retirement Portion

## Chapter Ten
### Interest & Compound Interest

## Chapter Eleven
### Stocks

## Chapter Twelve
### Certificates of Deposits (CDs)

## Chapter Thirteen
### United States Savings Bonds

## Chapter Fourteen
### Mutual Funds

# T of C (continued)

# Introduction

It is really great that you are taking the time to read this book. If it was given to you as a gift, be sure to thank the giver. If you picked it up yourself, you made a good decision. <u>How</u> you ended up with it is not the important part, what <u>is</u>, is reading and understanding the material in it. To get the most out of this book you must make sure that you understand what is being discussed as you move along because it builds upon the previous concepts discussed. If you do not understand an idea or example, **stop,** and figure it out. I know you can. Don't hesitate to ask someone or use the internet. As you move through this book you will find items mentioned that have been explained in previous chapters. Go back and review them if you do not remember the meaning. Each new concept will be thoroughly explained and usually will have an easy to understand example with it.

# Chapter One

## Why Read this Book

Why read this book?  EASY, when you are done with it you will know more about saving and investing your money than most of your peers.

Although frequently it is said that "money isn't important", don't believe it for a second. **MONEY IS IMPORTANT**.  I hope you heard me shout that, in case you didn't, Here is comes again.  MONEY IS IMPORTANT.  I did it softer that time because I knew you were expecting it.  Now it's your turn.

Say; <u>MONEY IS IMPORTANT</u> five times out loud.

This will become the basis for almost every concept, plan, or suggestion contained in this book. In case you're wondering why money is so important, just take a look around you. Just about every thing you see costs you or someone money. Even this book! Don't forget about some of the things that you cannot see such as electricity or whatever you and your family use to keep your house warm.

How about this thought? You began costing somebody money from the day you were born, probably even before you were born. Even before my sons were born, money was being spent to get ready for them, from clothes to furniture, and even for classes to help my wife and me get ready for the birth. Then there were the hospital expenses for each one and my wife. So you see, you have been using money in one way or another for quite some time.

There is something more important than money – **people**. Suze Orman, who is an expert on matters related to money, has a favorite saying that goes something like this; "People first – then money – then things." To me that means that no matter what, you must always be aware of other peoples feelings. You must always do the right thing, in this case meaning that you hurt no one, either emotionally or physically. You must always want to help out.

Back to the main purpose of this book, for you to grow up, live, and be a responsible and respected person, you must be able to manage your finances (money).

This adventure takes place through the following steps

## Getting money & Making money

## Saving money

## Investing money

## Using your money responsibly
## & staying out of debt

These are the core principles that you must fully understand. Each one of you needs to become experts with all aspects related to money. We will be starting out under the assumption that you are making money through a job, or at least an allowance.

A huge problem facing society today is debt, especially what is called "credit card debt". Debt is when you owe somebody something. For our purpose debt is any money that you need to pay back, either you borrowed money for something or you used somebody's money to buy something. Here are a couple of examples. The first is when you ask your parents for $100.00 to buy a new bicycle and you need to give them the $100.00 back at some point. The other one would be when you use a credit card. In this case you are using the credit card company's money to buy a new jacket. You get the jacket right away and you promise to pay the credit card company their money, the money that they paid for the jacket. We will have a whole chapter later on credit card debt.

Being a responsible, financially secure adult means having your debt under control. Better yet - HAVE NONE. In today's society, having only a car and house payment isn't too bad, as long as those payments are manageable. If you start saving now and continue to save and invest your money wisely you could even be able to avoid those payments.

We will start out discussing money and basic saving methods. We will then move on to investing. Which in this case means putting your money to work to make even more money.

# Chapter Two

## Money

When it comes to money I am sure that you know what it is, at least what it looks like, feels like, and tastes like (just kidding). You probably have a good idea how to spend it and hopefully know where it comes from. I am not talking about ATMs or the United States Mint either. In its simplest sense money is something that is exchanged for something. When you work for someone, money is given to you for the work that you do. When you buy a DVD you "trade" money for the DVD. Money is used because it is a convenient and mutually acceptable intermediate (in between) object for trading. Originally everything was bartered, or traded, one to one, when you needed something that you were not able to grow, make or do yourself. A doctor for example would be paid with a chicken or pig for helping out someone who was sick. A trapper could trade animal hides for a gun and so on. But, what if the trapper needed a canoe, I guess the trapper could find a canoe maker that needs a gun instead of pelts (hides). You get it? He trades the hides for a gun and then trades the gun for the canoe. Ok, let's take this one step further. What our trapper friend really needs is a cook stove. The stove maker does not need pelts, but, what he would like is a canoe. So ---- the trapper gets some animals and skins them, trades them for a gun, trades the gun for the canoe and trades the canoe for a cook stove. It works and everyone is happy, as long as all those involved are in need of the things that were available to trade. So now let's introduce money into our example. The trapper is good at trapping or hunting so that is what he does. He sells his pelts for money. He then buys his cook stove with money.  Money is a lot easier to carry around than a canoe.  Besides, what if he couldn't find a stove maker that needed a canoe?

So in the strictest sense money itself is useless, it is what we use it for that matters.  If one of your goals is to have "enough money to retire with", which should be one of your goals, it is not the money itself.  It is *what the money is needed for* when the time comes.  Unless of course you have stacks and stacks of the stuff and you are just going to burn it in your wood stove to keep warm.

Ok, so we agree that money is really only good to pay for the things that we want or need.  But here is an interesting zinger; money when managed correctly can "magically" grow itself into more money.  Just as planted seeds grow into large plants.  Come to think of it, what is the purpose of plants and trees – to make more plants and trees – right?  So, when you plant your money in good soil (by investing wisely), it will grow into more money.

Keep in mind that everyone has their own beliefs about money and all aspects related to money.  Let's look at a couple.  Where does money come from? To some people it just is always around and to others it is something to work hard for.  What do you do with your money? Save, invest, spend, and/or give?  Here is a tough one – what does money mean?  To some it means being able to or not being able to pay your bills.  To some it might be comforting to have and, believe it or not, some people are <u>not</u> comfortable having money.

It is important that you are comfortable in as many aspects as possible when it comes to money.  Here is what it all comes down to; you must be **knowledgeable** about the management of your money.  We will be learning about techniques for the proper management of money in future chapters.  And you need to be **decisive** regarding the management of your money.  This means that you are able to, and, that you do in fact make informed decisions about the management of your money in a timely fashion.  I was once told by someone that having a lot of money can ruin a church (or anything, or anybody, for that matter). I truly believe that it is the indecisive and improper handling of money that causes the demise.  We will learn that the real issue is that **not** having enough money <u>is the problem</u>.

# Chapter Three

## Saving Money

Why should you save your money?  If I was to present that question to a classroom of 30 of you guys, I would probably get about 10 or so answers the same and many more that you individually believe are important.

<u>On the next page are few of them</u>

To buy a car

Pay for college

Buy a computer type game

Go to the movies

New jeans

Hopefully even –"save for retirement"

And how about this one –"buy a house"

I'd love to hear – "to help out a charitable organization"

The truth is that there is usually more than one thing to save for.  The trick is how to divide your savings among the major categories.  What categories you might ask?  Well that is the first trick to proper saving.  First you will need to decide how many categories you will have.  In my earlier book, *GROW MONEY*, I suggested four categories.  To make it easy we set up jars and labeled them.  For you guys I suggest bigger jars or better yet coffee cans, as you will be putting in paper money as well as loose change. I will be suggesting four also for you to start with. If they work out right for you then stick with them. It is possible that when you finish this book and continue to become even more knowledgeable you may want to adjust your number of categories. The next important step is to stick with your savings categories distribution plan. Don't worry, not only does it become easy, but, there is even basic fun built in. Even more than the fun and satisfaction you will get watching the money grow.

Here are the categories for your four "cans"; SAVINGS, SPENDING, RETIREMENT, GIVING. It does not really matter how you label them, just somehow put these words on them. You could use a label maker, tape or just a marker. In a little bit we will discuss each container individually. Before that though, we need to decide how to allocate our funds. *Allocate* is just another word that means how, or, to distribute something, usually used when financial matters or money is concerned. Whenever you get any amount of money, it could be a gift, allowance or a paycheck, it needs to be divided and put into your cans. My suggestion for the percentage allocations are; GIVING 10%, SPENDING 30%, SAVING 30%, and RETIREMENT 30%. Just as a reminder on how percentages work, here is an example. For every dollar you need to allocate 10 cents into the giving jar, and allocate 30 cents into each of the spending, saving, and retirement containers. With ten dollars, it would be 1 dollar, 3 dollars, 3 dollars, and 3 dollars.

This has to be done every time, first thing, no matter what!

If you keep this up it will not take long before your containers are overflowing. You will need a plan to handle this situation.

# Chapter Four

## The GIVING concept

The GIVING container.   This is the money that you will give to worthwhile charitable organizations.  If you attend a religious service weekly you can take this money, all or some with you for the collection when you go.  Another idea is that you can wait until the end of the month and choose a recipient for your donation. It is important that by the end of the month this container <u>must</u> be emptied.

Wait a minute, if we are supposed to be saving money, why are giving it away?  I believe that there are a couple of very important reasons.  The first one is really simple – because it is the right thing to do.

There are many good people and organizations out there that are able to use your money to help those who are in need.  It really does make you feel good when you freely donate to a cause that you truly believe in.  The other is that by freely giving, giving to help others, miraculously you will find that you end up with even more money.  I have read and heard time and time again about this happening.  Here are a couple of stories.

I know this guy Bob who councils those who are having big problems with debt.  He tells of a husband and wife who owed a bunch of money.  Bob worked with them and set up a plan similar to our allocation cans.  They did great following the plan, paid off most of their debts and were moving along to becoming debt free.  In fact they were doing so good that they thought they could do even better by eliminating one of their allocation cans.  Can you guess which one?  They stopped filling their Giving can and therefore stopped donating to worthy causes. It did not take long before they were not able to put much money into the other containers. Once that happened they once again ended up having problems and fell back into debt.

Suze Orman, a famous author and financial planner uses this example (Suze, sorry about my adaptation). You could be very thirsty and standing at a water faucet without anything to catch the water to drink. If you put your closed fist under the water you will get nothing, if you open your hand you will get all the water you would like. What she means by all this is that if you open your hand to freely give, you will get what you want.

Here is another interesting example of the financial benefits of giving. I went down to Central America for a couple of weeks to help build a medical clinic up in the mountains. One of the guys that went down with our group is a very successful local businessman. We had lots of time to talk on the way down, all the way from New York and while there, no TV, radio or even electric. Somehow the conversation turned to charity and giving. He related to me that no matter how much money or services his family or business donated, he always would have enough money to pay his expenses and save for other things.

Many financial experts also agree about this phenomenon. I have found it to be true every single day. Because of the financial benefits and the emotional benefits, I never forget to take care of my giving. Here is the way that I learned that this works. Once upon a time(s), I would have a certain amount of money in my checking account. When spent on dumb things it seem to run out real quick, but, if I freely donated some to a worthwhile cause, I would still have enough money to cover my expenses and more! This sounds corny, but I see this and hear about this all of the time.

Keep in mind that you have something else to donate other than money. Just like you need to find worthy recipients of your giving money, you always are able to donate your time. When you donate your time, you will receive the same benefits as when you donate your money.

On the next page are some ideas:

Tutor (teach) a child

Help an elderly neighbor with yard work for free

Teach Sunday school

Grandpa or Grandma sit to help out an at home care provider

Help at a local blood drive

You might wonder sometimes if your money or your time really makes a difference. Here is a neat story about that very thing.

Wally Amos was walking along a beach one evening and noticed a man standing near the water. Although it was getting dark, he could see that the man was picking up and throwing things into the ocean. He was curious about what was going on so he walked over and saw that the man was picking up starfish and throwing them back into the sea. Wally asked him why he was doing that and this is what he was told. "You see the tide is out and these starfish will die up here on the beach." Wally tried to point out that it is getting dark and with thousands of miles of beach, there must be many, many starfish stranded. Wally asked the man if he really thought it was making a difference. As the man was throwing another out to sea, the man answered – "it does to that one."

Wally Amos by the way is the founder of the "Famous Amos" cookies that you may have heard of. I cannot say for sure if that is a true story. Maybe if Mr. Amos reads this book he will let me know. Whether or not it is true, the point is that in this world you really can make a difference, with one dollar, with one hour of your time, or even with one starfish.

# Chapter Five

## The Fun One

You will probably consider this, the SPENDING can, the most fun one. This is money that you get to spend now if you would like. Keep in mind that this does not mean that you <u>have</u> to spend it right away. This is your "on hand money". This is the money for movies, sodas, soccer games, candy and the like. If you are older and have a car, this would be your gas money. Speaking of gas money, even if you do not have your own car but you have friends that drive you around, you can always help them out with money for their gas. If you have parents that drive you around, you should also offer to help them out with the gas. This is especially true if they are driving you back and forth from a paying job. You have to realize that you are using their time and gas so that you can earn money. You might as well get used to it because sooner or later you will be paying for your own transportation.

Earlier I said that you don't have to spend it as soon as you get it. Here are a couple of examples if you spend unwisely. You go to a movie and have enough to buy your movie ticket but not enough to get a popcorn or box of raisinettes. How about this? You have enough money for your ticket but your friend is a little short. If you had not spent that extra couple of dollars the night before for the third slice of pizza that you really didn't need, you would have enough money to get you both into the movie. Remember, you cannot use your SAVING money; it is for bigger, special things.

Your SPEND container really is the most flexible portion of your distribution. Although the percentage of your money that goes in stays the same, how you use it is up to you. For example, you have been careful about your spending and notice that the can is almost full. Obviously you are not in need of all of this money for day to day expenses so you can move some to your other cans. I would suggest SAVINGS OR RETIREMENT. But there is no reason that it cannot go into your GIVING can. Remember though, that once the money is moved, it has to stay or be used according to the can or container that it is now placed.

# Chapter Six

## The Savings Portion

This is the container that will hold the money that you are saving for bigger, more expensive, and hopefully better items. First, we will talk about what these things might be and then how to put the money from this can to work so that it makes money on it's own.

More expensive items that you might not have enough money from your SPEND can might include things such as a new clothes, or electronics such as an

MP3 player. Even more expensive things might include a laptop or hunting equipment. Really expensive things could include a car or boat. These are things that will take a while to save for. You might have something in mind that you are saving for, or you might not. It is OK to just save your money, that way you will have it when you need it. There is a chance that you might come across an expensive thing that you need before you actually begin looking for it. For example, you have not turned old enough to drive a car yet so you have not even thought about looking for a car to buy. You have an uncle that is selling his car so that he can buy a pick-up truck. You and your parents know that it's a good car and has been well taken care of and would make a good first car for you. Because you have been good about saving, you just happen to have SAVED enough money to buy the car. If you didn't have the money ready, you uncle would have to sell his car to someone else. Later on when you planned on buying a car, you might not be able to find such a good car or at least such a good deal.

What about travel? Maybe there is a band trip coming up or you have a friend that is going to go someplace for vacation and you are invited to go. If you have the money available, you get to go. If not, you don't! It is as simple as that.

When you work for and save your money for something, it will mean more to you. You will appreciate and take better care of the item because you worked and saved for it. When I was in college I worked on an ambulance to pay my tuition. Even though I usually rode a city bus to get to work, sometimes I would have to drive. The only thing I was able to afford was an old broken down pick-up truck. It felt really good to look out of my dorm window and see my orange and red truck. Frequently, I did not have enough money to buy gas for it, but it was mine and I had worked and saved all the money to pay for it. I did that by working in a nuclear power plant, but that is another story. A friend of mine at school had a new Mustang for a car. Even though she had a really nice and expensive car, she didn't care about it all. Why? You guessed it; she didn't work for the money to buy it herself. Her parents bought her the car and even paid for the gas that she put in it. I tried to explain to her how good it felt to have earned and paid for my truck but she did not, or could not, understand. When I saved enough money to buy a new truck, I was able to decide when, and whom, to sell my pick-up truck to because it was really mine.

# Chapter Seven

## Retirement

We will use the term "retirement" to mean when a person is done with having to work for a living. It can happen when they *decide to* or *when they have to*, usually because they have reached a certain age. Many people really look forward to the time that they are able to retire so that they can relax, go on vacations, or just be able to do the things that they never had time for while they had to work to support themselves or their families.

Years ago, very little planning went into being able to retire.  People would work for one "large" company for a long time and when they were old enough they would stop working.  It used to be that most people worked for large companies, factories, or the government.  Nowadays, not only are there more smaller companies, but people tend to change jobs often.  The frequent changing of jobs means that an individual does not work for any one company for enough years to earn a "pension".  A *pension* is the money that you would get paid after you retire.  As far as smaller companies go, for the most part, they have very limited abilities to pay a significant pension for those who retire.

Think about this.  Suppose you owned a small company, let's say with 20 people, making one small part for jets that the Air Force uses. After a few years some of your employees are getting too old to do their job and want to retire.  The way it works is that the Air Force (actually a big company working for the Air Force) pays you a certain amount of money for each part that you make and deliver.  You in turn have to pay your employees, usually by the hour or it could be by the number of parts they make or a set amount per year, which is called a "salary."  <u>And</u>, you have to make enough money for yourself and enough to cover the expenses involved in running a business.  And of course, you have to spend a large amount of the money coming in to make the parts.  Some of the bigger expenses include buying the raw materials, paying your employees and don't forget the electric and gas company needs to be paid also.  And don't forget you have to pay yourself and the many other expenses involved in running a business, things like ink for the printers and toilet paper for the restrooms (washrooms, for our Canadian friends).  All of these things go into the making the parts to make money to keep your operation going on a daily basis.  The word *overhead* is generally used to describe all of the costs involved in running a business

So back to the retirement/pension thing, you have employees that want to, have to, or have retired, and of course they want to still get money (at least some) from you for working for your company for awhile.  Here is what it comes down to if you do not have a ton of money laying around.  Do you pay the employees that are still working and making the parts to sell to make money for the company or pay the employees that are not working anymore? It would be great to be able to do both, but that is not always the case. So of course you have to pay the employees which you need to keep making aircraft parts, which leaves little for those not contributing to your business.

So you see. An "automatic" pension to pay you after you stop working is not "automatic" anymore. Smaller companies may not have the means to do it. Your generation has become very mobile. In this case, meaning moving and changing jobs often. Because of these factors, you need to take care of your retirement needs while you are working.

Health insurance is another "automatic" benefit that is not always provided, at least not for free, for many of the same reasons. So keep health insurance needs in mind also.

# Chapter Eight

## Social Security

Ok, so a pension is not guaranteed anymore, what about that thing called "social security"? First, what is social security? *Social Security* is a program that was set up by the United States government, signed by then President Franklin Roosevelt in 1935, to make sure that people would have enough money to live on once they were either too old or physically unable to work. At that time over 50% of senior citizens were living below the poverty level. In other words, they were not able to afford the basic things to live. To collect the money needed for this program, employers are required to give the government a portion of the money that their employees earn, as well as some of their own. The government holds this money until the employee is eligible, or able, to begin to get it back in payments. It wasn't a bad idea and has worked for many years. But, and this is a big BUT, the amount of money held by the social security administration is being paid out faster than it is going in.

Ponder this, in 1940 Social Security paid out 35 million dollars. In 2004 it paid out over 500 BILLION dollars.

Think of it this way, you have a bucket that you are trying to put water into and your bucket has a hole in it. If you could not put water in as fast or faster than the water was running out through the hole, the level of water would keep getting lower until the bucket had no water in it because the water running out was more than what you were putting in.

# Got it ???

As far as social security goes, here is what's happening. First, people are being required to be older to begin collecting. As of this writing you would get a partial payment at age 62, but not your full payment until age 70. This is an attempt to slow the flow of money out. Second, payments are smaller (percentage wise). And lastly, and maybe the most significant, with more and more people living longer than before, more and more money is being paid out. Using our bucket example, like the water, more money is leaving than is being put into the bucket, or in this case the social security fund. In fact, some estimate at the current and projected rate that the money is being paid out and what is going in, that in the year 2050 only 75% of claims will be able to be paid. From then on payments will decrease for some time.

So -- if a pension is not guaranteed to provide money for retirement, and Social Security is running out of money, how will you have the money for the things you will need after you retire? Meaning, necessities such as being able to buy food, medicine or the other things you really need, and what about the things that you would *like* to do. Things like travel, or in my case live in a cabin in the woods with my wife.

So -- how can you be ready for the time in your life when you want, notice that I said <u>want</u> **not** <u>need</u>, to retire?  Read on McDuff.  Who's McDuff you ask? What just happened is an attempt at humor with a play on words, you see there is a saying out there "Lead on McDuff".  Get it? *Read* on McDuff - *Lead* on McDuff.  If you got it, great.  If not, forget it, it has absolutely nothing to do with money. In any case just keep reading for the answer.

# Chapter Nine

## The RETIREMENT Portion

Ok, so if you cannot count on a pension from a company that you have worked for, and you definitely cannot count on enough (if anything at all) from the government, here is the answer. It is fairly simple. You have to TAKE CARE OF IT YOURSELF. This means that you have to save and invest wisely for your retirement. I know it seems like it is a long time away, but trust me before you know it you will decide that <u>you</u> <u>want</u> to retire.

The first step is to set aside the portion of your money, from now on we will refer to your "coming in money" as *income*, for retirement. Earlier I suggested that 30 percent of any income that you have be set aside for retirement. Remember in this case, your retirement portion; even more than the others is really a two step process. First is the setting aside or the *saving* step. The second step involves proper *investing*. You see by starting early you have the advantage of time. Meaning, you will have many years before needing your retirement money. Properly investing your money will allow your money to grow on its own. In other words, your money can work to make you more money. In fact, once you have saved and invested enough money, your money could actually be making more money on its own than you are saving from your income. Pretty cool, huh?

You have the saving part down. Now let's work on the investing part. The next few chapters will deal with investment techniques. We will hit the extremes in the next two chapters. First, in Chapter 10, the way that protects your investment the most will be discussed, known as *low risk*.

The next chapter, Chapter 11, you will learn about the riskiest way to invest. After dealing with the risk extremes we will work on a couple of ways to invest in the middle of the risk range.

# Chapter Ten

## Interest & Compound Interest

The first, and by far the easiest and most secure way of investing, is using the concept of compound interest. Easy because it is automatic, you put in, or *deposit*, your money into a bank account. Once you have deposited your money it will grow, but more about that in a second. Being *secure* means that no matter what is happening, or has happened, in this country, the world, or the money business (sounds like another old saying – monkey business – doesn't it?

But I won't go into that one) you will not have to worry about losing your deposited money.

Before we talk about the amazing thing called "compound interest" we have to first discuss "interest." *Interest* is what is paid to use someone else's money. There are two kinds. First is the kind that you have to pay because you are using, or borrowing, someone's or something's, like a bank's, money. The other kind is the kind that someone or some organization, like a bank, pays you because they are using your money.

For now let's stick with the good kind of interest, the kind that gets paid to you. Rest assured in time we will get to the bad kind, which is the kind you have to pay.

When you deposit money into your bank account, you are letting the bank use your money. In return the bank pays you interest. You are probably wondering as to what the bank does with that money. It uses your money as well as the deposits of others to make more money. Make as in earn, not as in printing it, which is the job of the government. So here is how *compound interest* works. You deposit one hundred dollars into your bank account. Depending on your bank they will pay you your interest monthly, quarterly or yearly, usually monthly or quarterly, for this example, we will figure monthly. Also, let's assume that your bank is paying five percent (5%) interest monthly. In the real world, the posted rate would be yearly. Ok, so you deposit $100.00. At the end of your first month you will have the $100.00 that you deposited PLUS the $5.00 of interest that the bank paid you for a total of $105.00. Pretty cool, huh, but it gets better. So the next month starts with $105.00 and you would then get $5.25 at the end of the month for a total of $110.25. We will go one more for this example. The next month you start with $110.25 and you would get $5.51 in interest for a total of $115.76.

And that is the magic of compound interest. Time and some money is all it takes. Keep in mind that in our example we deposited money only once. Your bank account will grow even faster with regular deposits. The more money that is in your account, the larger chunks of interest the bank pays, and keeps paying, you. Take a look at the following chart to see another example. Currently some of the best interest rates are being found with online banks, but they are not as convenient for deposits and withdrawals as working with a local bank in your own neighborhood.

On the next page is a chart that shows what

happens if you save and invest just 50 cents

a day for 25 years and you are earning

10 % compounded interest

| Year | Balance | Year | Balance |
|------|---------|------|---------|
| 1 | $ 188.48 | 13 | $ 4,769.25 |
| 2 | $ 396.70 | 14 | $ 5,457.14 |
| 3 | $ 626.73 | 15 | $ 6,217.06 |
| 4 | $ 880.84 | 16 | $ 7,056.55 |
| 5 | $ 1,161.56 | 17 | $ 7,983.94 |
| 6 | $ 1,471.67 | 18 | $ 9,008.45 |
| 7 | $ 1,814.26 | 19 | $ 10,140.23 |
| 8 | $ 2,192.72 | 20 | $ 11,390.53 |
| 9 | $ 2,610.81 | 21 | $ 12,771.75 |
| 10 | $ 3,072.67 | 22 | $ 14,297.61 |
| 11 | $ 3,582.91 | 23 | $ 15,983.24 |
| 12 | $ 4,146.57 | 24 | $ 17,845.37 |
| | | **25** | **$ 19,902.50** |

# Chapter Eleven

## Stocks

If a savings account is the <u>most</u> secure way of investing, something must be the <u>least</u> secure. For our purposes we will say that owning individual stocks carry the most risk. Meaning that if things go bad you could lose some or all of your money. There are other investment techniques that are very complicated and even more risky, but those are only for those who know tons about them. Guess what? I am not one of them. So we will stick with stocks.

What are stocks?  When you buy a *stock* you are actually buying a part of a company.  In other words you become a part owner of that company.  Being an owner means that if things are going well for that particular business you will make money.  What happens if things are not going so well?  You guessed it!  You can or will lose money.

There are two and a half ways to make (hopefully) money with stocks. First is with an increase in the individual price of the stock.  The next is through dividends.  And the half – through stock splits.

## ---- Stock Prices ----

Here is how it works.  Say for instance you want to buy stock in the Coke company.  As to how to actually buy it, you will find it at the end of this chapter.  I have rounded the numbers to simplify this example.  You happened to have $60.00 to invest and you think that since you drink a lot of Cherry Coke (which is made by Coca-Cola) you might as well own part of that company.  Although that alone is a really cool thing, we are here about investing.  Choosing stocks in the companies that you and your friends use is a great way to start investing. Especially if you believe that things are going well for them. Remember though that even if you like a certain brand of sneakers, for example, but heard that they are going out of business, as far as investing goes, don't buy their stock!

Back to your $60.00. You go on the internet and find out that the current price of Coke stock is $50.00 per share. A *share* is a part of the company. You have enough money to buy one "1" share, so you do. Congratulations, new owner of Coke, drink up. Other than you and your friends drinking an extra million cans of pop (soda, depending on where you live) or so, how will you make money with your one share of stock. There are two ways, wait, two and a half. The first is that after you bought your share at $50.00, the price goes up. To make it easy, and good for you, let's say to $60.00 per share. If you were to sell your share for $60.00 and it originally cost you $50.00 you just made yourself $10.00. Now for the bad possibility, if you sell your stock and the current price has gone down to $40.00 per share, and you paid $50.00 you will have lost $10.00.  That is why owning individual stocks are risky.  You can make money or you can lose money.

Think about this for a moment, What if you bought 100 shares instead of 1?  The results, both ways, would be a hundred times different.  Meaning, if the price had gone up by $10.00 per share, you would have made $1000.00.  BUT, if the price had gone down by $10.00 you would have lost $1000.00.

Here is another thing you need to think about.  Should you buy a few shares of a more expensive stock or many shares of a lower price stock?  This is a tough one.  People that are "experts", or at least educated, in stock matters will have different opinions on this choice.  Generally, but not always, the more expensive stocks are those of larger well established companies.  They usually will have a proven record of being in business and doing business.  Since we're talking about investing and are still on the first way to make money with stocks, we need to look at how the changes in the stock price works for those options.  One or a few higher priced stocks or many shares of a lower price stock.

Let us assume that whichever stock or stocks that you buy, the price per share goes up by $1.00. If you bought 50 shares of a company at the cost of $1.00 per share for $50.00 and the price went up $1.00, to $2.00 a share and you then sold your stock, you would have made $50.00

Look at this example this way:

Bought 50 shares x $1.00 per share = $50.00
Sold 50 shares x $2.00 per share = $100.00

$100.00 (sold for) - $50.00 (bought for) =

**$50.00 profit**

Here is the same example using a higher priced stock. You have the same $50.00 to invest in the stock market. You purchase a stock that cost $50.00. Since you only have $50.00 to invest you are able to by only one share. The price once again goes up $1.00 per share, in this case to $51.00.

Look at this example this time:

Bought 1 share x $50.00 per share = $50.00

Sold 1 share x $51.00 per share = $51.00

$51.00 (sold for) - $50.00 (bought for) =

**$1.00 profit**

Big difference right? There sure is. But there are a bunch of things to keep in mind. To start with for a cheap stock to double in price (as in our example) is very, very rare. Stocks selling in the dollar range may only move a few cents at a time. On the other hand expensive stocks (like over $100.00 per share) can jump (up or down) by many dollars at a time. Always keep in mind that stock prices can move up OR down at any given time. Many factors affect the stock price; the company's business operation, orders (or cancelled orders) for their product and even world or national events.

The best thing you can do is to learn as much as possible about the companies of which you are considering buying stock in. Find companies that have a good product or service and a realistic growth plan for the future. Stocks should be purchased for the long run. Meaning, you should plan on keeping the stock for many years. There are people who buy and then sell the stock in a short period of time. They are called "*day traders*". Day trading is a very risky way to deal with stocks.

## ---- Stock Dividends ----

A *dividend* is when a company gives some of its profit to the owners. Remember that as a *stockholder*, meaning that you own some of their stock, you are a part owner. Dividends are paid to you per share of stock that you own. The more shares you own, the more money that is paid to you, usually quarterly or monthly. Not all companies pay dividends. Whether or not a company pays dividends is something you need to think about when considering buying stock. It is not a huge deal at this point, but you should at least consider it. Most companies offer what is called a *dividend reinvestment* program. What happens is that instead of sending you a check for the dividend, the money is put back in to buy you more shares.  It is automatic and a very good idea at your stage of investing.

# ---- Stock Splits ---

## (The "Half")

A *stock split is* what happens when a company decides that they want to change the number of shares that are out there.  There are two main reasons that they might want to do this.  Usually it is done to alter the current stock price, the other is strictly to change the number of shares that the company either still holds (owns themselves) or that the stockholders own. The reasons for changing the numbers of shares in existence are numerous and complicated, and we will not be going into them.  We will however discuss how stock spits affect the current price of the stock.

Sometimes the price of a stock keeps working its way up until it become very expensive, like a hundred dollars or more.  When a stock becomes very expensive many average investors are unable to afford to buy the stock.  Some companies like to keep their stock affordable so the way to bring the price back down is a stock split. During a stock split is the only time that it is good for the price of a stock we own to go down. Here's why. We will start with what would be called a 2 for 1 split. There could be others such as 3 to 1, or 4 to 1, or even other combinations. In a 2 for 1 split (this is pretty easy) you end up with 2 shares for every one share that you own. As far as the price goes, at the time of the split the cost of each share in a 2 for 1 split is cut in half. So if you own 20 shares selling for let's say $10.00 per share, your stock is worth $200.00 before the split. Immediately after the split you would then own 40 shares selling for $5.00 per share, your stock is still worth $200.00.

Look at it this way:

Before the split

20 shares x $10.00 per share = $200.00

After the split

40 shares x $5.00 per share = $200.00

You see although you, and everybody else that owns this stock, has twice as many shares the price ends up cut in half.  That is why the value stays the same.  So how do stock splits help you make money? Sticking with our same numbers form this example, the original price was $10.00 per share, right?  Say RIGHT. After the split the price was $5.00 per share, right? RIGHT?  Here it comes, there are probably many investors who would have liked to buy the stock but originally felt that it was too expensive at $10.00 per share.  Now the stock is selling for only $5.00 per share.  They think "wow – what a bargain" and start buying up the stock.  When a lot of people are buying a particular stock, the price per share goes up.  As an example, let us suppose that the price goes up to $7.00 (up $2.00) per share

In other words:

Before the split
20 shares x $10.00 per share = $200.00

After the split
40 shares x $5.00 per share = $200.00

Some time later

40 shares x $7.00 per share = $280.00

Usually, but not always, stock prices will go up after a split so they can be good overall. I once had a stockbroker that always answered the same way when I asked him if a particular stock was going to, or possibly, split. His answer was "... it doesn't matter, so you end up with twice as many shares of stocks that are worth half as much." That is true at the time of the split, but, as I said before, the price usually goes up after a split. Sometimes a company will split their stock over and over again. There are people around that may have purchased just a few shares of a stock 75 years ago that have now turned into hundreds, if not thousands of shares. So just like in compound interest, time becomes a great helper in helping you to grow money using stocks.

Since we are on the topic of stock splits, there is also a process called a reverse stock split. Like 1 for 2, 2 for 3, or even 1 for 100. There are times when a company wants to reduce the number of shares available. One of the reasons is if the stock price is falling and the company wants to keep the price up there.  Why?  Like anything else in this world if something is too cheap it is perceived, or thought, to be not very good.  Also, stocks that trade i.e. buy or sell, for less that $1.00 per share are treated differently by brokerage firms or the services that keep track of publicly traded companies.  *Publicly traded companies* are the businesses of which you can buy and sell their stock.

Here we go again, keeping our numbers the same for simplicity:

Before the split

20 shares x $10.00 per share = $200.00

After the split

10 shares x $20.00 per share = $200.00

# - Buying and Selling Stocks –

How can you buy individual stocks? There are 3 main ways. First, is to establish an account with a local stockbroker. A *stockbroker* is someone who can buy or sell the stocks you tell him or her to buy or sell. Second, is to establish an account with an online brokerage firm. A *brokerage firm* is a company that will process your orders for the purchase or sale of stock. I know you know what online means. Third, is to buy very small numbers of stock from online companies that specialize in the sale of one or two shares at a time. Just use your favorite search engine to find one online, there are a few.

# Chapter Twelve

## Certificates of Deposits (CDs)

Certificates of deposits (CDs) are another safe way to invest. Usually they are done through banks, although investment companies and even churches can get involved. An organization, such as a church, can utilize CDs to raise money from the members of the congregation for some large *capital*, meaning building, project. The way that a CD works is that you buy one for whatever amount of money you would like, however sometimes there is a minimum amount that you need to invest. The amount of interest and the amount of time is set from the start. For example, you could buy a $1000.00 CD that matures in 18 months and will pay 6% interest. *Mature* means the amount of time that it will take for you to receive your full interest amount. Frequently banks will charge a "penalty" if you take your money out early. Generally the interest rates are better than a savings account, but, in return, your money is "tied up" for a set amount of time. With a savings account you can withdraw your money at any time.

# Chapter Thirteen

## United States Savings Bonds

United States Savings Bonds are similar to CDs except they are issued by, you guessed it, the United States Government. When you buy a savings bond, you buy it for half the face value. *Face value* is the amount that is printed in the bond itself. For example, you would buy a $50.00 savings bond for $25.00. The next question you should be thinking about is "if I buy the bond at half the face value, when does it become worth what it says on it?" The answer used to be an easy one – 7 years – but not anymore. There are now a couple of different types available, and they all use an adjustable time frame and interest rate to reach maturity. In this case *maturity* means that they reach the printed face value. I suggest that if you would like to invest in savings bonds that you sit down with one of the people at your bank that sits at a desk, not a teller, which are the people at the counter. They will explain the current rates and time frames with you. The easiest way to purchase savings bonds is through your own bank. The rates are generally better than CDs and are backed by the United States government.

What, you may ask, is the government doing with your money that you are letting them use? Running and taking care of the country. Savings bonds would be considered another fairly safe investment. Like CDs your money will be tied up for a while. One last thing to remember about savings bonds, the bonds themselves are needed for *redemption,* meaning to get your money back out, and are very difficult to replace. You have to have them for a long time, 6 or more years. They have to be protected from damage or loss. This would be a good time to look into a bank safety deposit box. A *safety deposit box* is rented from the bank and is kept locked up in their big vault. Another option would be to encourage your family to get a good quality fire rated safe to keep all of the family's important papers in.

# Chapter Fourteen

## Mutual Funds

Mutual Funds are collections of either stocks or some other type of investments. The key word here is "collection". Usually this collection has something in common. For example, a technical fund would probably be comprised of stocks from companies that make, you guessed it, technical things such as computers or electronic components. The companies could also be providers of some sort of technical service such as internet or even web based service providers such as Google or AOL.  Another group of investments that could make up a Mutual Fund are bonds, either issued by the United States government, state government, local government and/or even individual companies.  There are many others but these are the most common.

**Fun Fact** -Two hundred folks invested $ 392,000 in March of 1924 to establish the first mutual fund, which was called the Massachusetts Investors Trust. As of October 2007 there were 8015 mutual funds with total combined assets of over 12 TRILLION DOLLARS.

| March 1924 | 1 Mutual Fund | $ 392,000 |
| October 2007 | 8015 Mutual Funds | $12,356,000,000,000 |

OK, so why a collection instead of just one company or bond? Because, stocks, and even some bonds are considered or known to be volatile.  *Volatile* in this case means that the price, or value, can change by a lot.  When they go up it is usually a good thing because your investment amount will increase.  When they go down you will lose money.  This could be the money that you have "made" in the past or it could even be all or part of the money that you put in (i.e. invested). By having a bunch of different stocks or bonds together in a group like this, your chances are better that even though at times some will decrease in value, enough will increase in value over time so that the overall value of the entire mutual fund increases.

There are different levels of volatility among mutual funds. Some would be considered "safer" than others. *Safer* meaning that it is less likely that you will lose your investment. So if some mutual funds are "safe", and some funds carry enough risk that you could lose money, why would you, or anyone for that matter, put their money in a higher risk fund? The answer is that along with the increased risk of not making or even losing money, is the possibility of making larger - and sometimes quicker – sums of money.

Just in case you are wondering, and you should be, how does the value of a mutual find change, let me explain. Remember that the funds are made of stocks and/or bonds. Each stock or bond has the ability to increase in value or decrease in value. So at any given time if the majority of the stocks or bonds are increasing in value (or making money) then the overall fund will be increasing in value. Conversely, if the majority of the stocks or bonds are <u>decreasing</u> in value then the overall fund will be decreasing in value. The thought is, and the hope is, that by having a bunch stocks or bonds that the making money ones will outnumber the losing ones.

The next logical question is then – how and/or why does the value (price) of the individual stocks or bonds change? We covered stocks in Chapter 11, if you don't remember, jump back and read it again. As far as bonds go, the simplest way to illustrate it involves the *concept of supply and demand*. The way that the **concept of supply and demand** works is that when more people want a limited supply of a thing, the price of that item can and will increase. This is also known as a *sellers market*. Conversely, if the supply of something is large and not many people want it, the price will decrease. This case is known as a *buyers market.* Another factor involves the interest rates that banks use among themselves, so to speak, which is set by the government.

I want you to think about the sellers/buyers market terms and see if you can figure it out – that is who is benefiting from each situation.

# Chapter Fifteen

## Supply & Demand and Worth

Let's go through this again because this concept is very important and works its way into our lives all of the time and will continue to do so. When you're in college and take an economics class you will get to learn all about widgets. What!!! You don't know what a widget is? A widget is a thing. You get it now? Oh, you want to know what thing is a widget. OK I'll tell you. A *widget* is an imaginary thing that people want (or may not want). Although no one thing is a widget, widgets are an important part of learning about economics. As far as we're concerned, *economics* is the way money works within a specific culture. A more precise definition is that Economics is the study of the production, distribution, and consumption of goods and services.

Back to widgets, if a company makes a set number of widgets, set because their factory can only manufacture a certain number of widgets because of production issues or maybe there are just not enough raw materials available. In this case let us assume that many, many people want them, what do you think will happen to the price of widgets. Do you think that the price will go up, stay the same, or go down?

Now let us think about this. If the same factory makes the same number of widgets and very few people want, or even care about widgets, what will then happen to the cost of each widget? Same question, do you think that the price will go up, stay the same, or go up.

Now before I answer the questions, although I am sure that you have the right answers already, I need to make something very clear. This is one of the most important lessons in this book and in life.

# Things are worth what people are willing to pay for it, or them

For example, let us assume that you own a house, a house that you bought 10 years ago for $100,000. Over the years, while you lived in it, you fixed it up and added some things to it like an alarm system, new flooring and a swimming pool. You have kept good records on what you spent improving your house. Actually, you should keep these records because you WILL need them for tax reasons when you sell your house.

Now you have decided that it is time to sell the house. So how much should you try to sell it for? In other words, are you ready - what is it worth? Let's say that to start with you know that you paid $100,000 for it, and the pool, flooring, and security system added together cost $30.000. That brings the total to $130,000. Does that mean that your house is worth $130,000? Not necessarily. Remember <u>you</u> paid $100,000 for the house 10 years ago and <u>you</u> paid $30,000 for improvements.

***The house is worth what someone else is willing to pay for it.  And not a penny more!!!***

If the going rate for a house in your area is much higher now, and someone was looking for a house in that area that likes to swim they might be willing to pay, let's say $200,000.  In this case you will have made money, or in financial terms, your investment appreciated.

However, it can work the other way also.  If houses in the area are selling for less, the amount that you might be offered would be less.  As for that pool that you installed, if the potential buyer is not interested in pools, having a pool could cause the price to be lower.  Maybe the best price offered is $90,000. In this case your investment has depreciated.

***The house is worth what someone else is willing to pay for it.  And not a penny more !!!***

Back to widgets.  The answer to the questions, in case you did not figure them out on your own, are directly affected by the concept of supply & demand, which we talked about at the beginning of this chapter. Simply put, supply & demand means that when you have more people wanting (demand) something (supply) and the number wanting is higher the amount available, the price people are willing to (or have to) pay will go up. The opposite is also true. If there is a lot of something available the price will go down.

Here is a simple, and somewhat silly, example.

Gold, there is not a lot of it around so people are willing to pay a lot for it. Dirt on the other hand is plentiful. The price, or in this case *value*, of gold will be much higher than dirt. Got it???

So don't forget this:

# Things are worth what people are willing to pay for it, or them

# Chapter Sixteen

## Mutual Fund Basics

### Types of Funds

Now that you have a basic understanding as to what a mutual fund is, how do you decide which way to go when choosing a mutual fund to invest in? Earlier we discussed volatility regarding investments and how volatility affects gains or losses. There is another important factor to consider with mutual funds, and that is – TIME. Not the time of the day but the amount of time you can hold onto the mutual fund.

Historically most funds over a long period of time will increase in value. Some funds, the volatile ones, can increase in shorter periods of time. BUT these volatile funds are more likely to go down in value than the more stable ones. Another way this is said in the financial world would be to use terms like *more aggressive and less aggressive*. A more aggressive mutual fund will include stocks from usually smaller companies that have potential for faster growth. However these smaller companies have increased risk of failure because being smaller, and sometimes younger they may not have the whole business thing figured out yet. When they do work out, they usually do so quicker which increase the value of their stock which in turn increases the value of the mutual fund.

The same goes for a mutual fund which holds bonds instead of stocks. Bonds that are issued for longer periods of time from established companies or the government (local, state or national) are considered less aggressive. In this case, less aggressive meaning that they are less likely to lose value. A more aggressive bond fund will hold bonds from smaller agencies that although they might increase in value quicker, may not have the reputation or ability to pay the money back.

Here is an example:

Let's assume that you are a city and need to raise money by selling some bonds. Remember that a bond is something that someone buys, and after some time the bond is turned in for the original amount plus some extra money. If you (the city) has a good reputation for paying back its loans many people are willing to buy your bonds. Remember supply & demand. If there are many people wanting your bonds, you do not have to offer them much extra money to buy your bonds. On the other hand if you (still the city) are not trusted as much to pay back your loans (in this case – the bonds), not as many people want your bonds. To get them to buy your bonds, you have to offer to pay them back either sooner or with more extra money.

The same goes for stocks. A company like IBM has been around for a long time. People assume that IBM knows how to run a company and has lots of assets. *Assets* are things of value, including money.

Because they are trusted, people are willing to buy their stocks because they will continue to make money over time. Stocks in smaller companies, younger companies or ones with fewer assets may not be as trusted. To entice people to by their stock they have to promise more (dividends for example) or have the potential to grow over a short period of time. Unfortunately, sometimes these companies do not grow or survive.

Back to the first question of this chapter. How do you choose a mutual fund? This one does not get an "easy" answer. In fact it depends on a bunch of things. Two of the most important concepts are:

**Risk** – How willing are you take a chance that you will lose some or all of you investment.

**Time** – How much time do you have to let your investment grow?

Assuming that you are fairly young, although you may not consider being a teenager that young, you really are, you have a lot of time for your investments to grow. This is a good thing. This also means that should you choose to invest in less risky or less aggressive things, they have the time to cruise along on their merry way toward growth. Have you heard the saying "slow and steady wins the race"? It has to do with the tortoise and the hare story. If it does not sound familiar go look it up and read the story.

Now let us say that you choose to invest in risky or more aggressive investments. Although they may from time to time go down in value, over time they will probably increase in value.

When it comes to mutual fund investing, the <u>time</u> that you, being a young investor, have will be of a huge advantage towards becoming financially secure. Don't ever forget that money <u>is</u> important.

Ok, so what collection of stocks (or bonds) should you buy? It really is up to you. Everybody has their own opinion. Like the saying goes about opinions, *everyone has one just like an elbow*. Never heard that one before, just ask a trucker.

Back in Chapter 14 we talked about a couple of examples of a couple of collections in mutual funds. So if YOU believe that technical things are cool and will make you money in the long run, buy technical mutual funds. If you think more people in the future will be taking cruises and going to fancy hotels and resorts, then a "leisure time" oriented mutual fund would be a good choice.

There are so many collections that you have to find the one that works for you. Presently there is a new group of mutual funds that are referred to as "lifestyle funds". *Lifestyle funds* hold a collection of stocks (and sometimes stocks and bonds) balanced in such a way to grow in value over a longer period of time with relatively low risk. Investors in lifestyle funds need to review their fund and adjust the types of units held to meet their future retirement plans.

Speaking of risk, risk is the other thing that you have to decide. How much risk are you willing to take with your money? Usually with time on your side, riskier funds are a reasonable choice. When you get much older and are getting close to needing the money that you have invested, it is best to move the money to a less risky investment. Why - because of our friend TIME. Remember that when time was on your side, losses could be made up. If TIME is short, losses may not be made up before you need, or want, to use your investment.

There are two other important terms and concepts to understand when choosing a mutual fund. One is load. The *load* associated with a mutual fund refers to how the people that administer the fund are paid for their expertise and time.

With a front load fund a portion of your investment comes out of your investment at the beginning each time you invest. For example, depending on the percentage charged, if you have $100.00 to invest, $10.00 could go to the mutual fund company as pay and $90.00 would go into your investment.

With a rear, or end load, fund the fees are deducted from the money that you take out. For example, you call, or email, your mutual fund company and tell them that you want to take out $100.00 from your fund. You probably can see where this is going. $100.00 comes out of your investment, $10.00 goes to the company, and $90.00 is sent to you.

And lastly, as far as loads go, are what are called *no-load* funds. These do not take any money away at the time of investment or when money is taken out. So how does the organization administering the fund get paid? After all they are a business and are entitled to make money.  They take their administrative fees out of the day to day money being generated within the fund.  This means that if you invest $100.00, all $100.00 goes into you fund.  And of course if you request $100.00, you will be sent $100.00.

So if you are still with me, you are probably wondering why anyone would use anything but a no-load fund.  Frequently, but not always, loaded funds seem to do better, although sometimes the numbers are deceiving because of accounting practices.  Also, professional investors feel that with loaded funds, a better, in this case meaning more accurate, assessment of the funds performance can assessed. For the average investor like you or me at this point, I recommend sticking with a no-load mutual fund.

The last factor to consider is whether to choose a fund that is taxable, non-taxable or tax deferred. Better put your seatbelt on for this one.

A taxable fund is a fund that you put in money that has been taxed already.  The money that your fund makes each year is also taxed.

A non-taxable (or tax sheltered) fund uses the taxed money that you invest to purchase things, bonds usually, that are not taxable when they increase in value, or when you take your money out.

A tax deferred mutual fund uses your money that has not been taxed to invest in things that may or may not be taxable as they grow. You are not taxed each year. Money has to go straight from your employer to the mutual fund administrator. When you take the money out you are taxed on both the original money as well as the money that is generated within the fund. There are two major advantages of this type of fund. First, you are actually making money on all of your money that goes into the fund. And when you take this money out when you are much older, the thought is that you will be required to pay a smaller percentage of tax. This type of fund works best for investing money to be used to support you during retirement.

# Chapter Diecisiete

## Choosing a Mutual Fund

Ok, now let's review the mutual fund terms that you now understand. If you do not fully understand them, review the previous chapter, if you still are having trouble please take some time to find some help. We have discussed the three main types of mutual funds as related to load; front load, end load, and no load. Next we went over how taxable, tax sheltered, and tax deferred mutual funds are taxed. So with that understanding, let us proceed with how to choose the one for you to invest in.

As far as "load" goes, as I mentioned before, my recommendation for people like us are "no-load" funds. Remember those are the ones that put your entire contribution into the fund. So what about the taxing options? Unless you are working and get a regular paycheck, you will not be able to use the tax deferred one with untaxed dollars, which leaves the two choices that use already taxed money. You need to then make the decision whether you want to be taxed each year or not taxed. Of course it sounds better to earn money that will not be taxed, because you get to keep more of the money that the mutual fund earns. Right? Right. Here is the kicker though. Usually taxed funds earn a larger percentage that un-taxed.

Let us compare a couple of funds. Fund A is a conventional no-load taxable fund. Fund A usually earns about 12 percent per year. Fund B, a tax free no-load fund earns about 8 percent per year. Based on this information only which one would you choose. Certainly Fund A would make you more money than B, in this case about 4 percent more. BUT that 12 percent that you are making is taxed by the state and federal (United States) governments. Let's go with a couple of different tax rates. If the total taxes on your earned money is 5 percent, which is better? Fund A with its 12 percent gain minus the 5 percent tax equals a 7 percent gain. Fund B, not taxable earned you 8 percent. So in this case Fund B would be a better choice – get it? What if the tax rate was 2 percent? Fund A (12 percent) minus 2 percent equals 10 percent. Even being taxed you would get to keep 2 percent more than with Fund B.

This time we will keep the tax rate the same at 5 percent. If Fund A usually earns, say 15 percent, you will still be a further ahead than using the tax sheltered Fund B.

Usually, there's that word again, conventional (taxed) mutual funds outperform non-taxable ones. *Outperform* in this case means does better. So taking this into account, a conventional, taxed, mutual fund is a reasonable choice for the average investor. In case you are wondering who would benefit from a non-taxable fund, it would be for people who pay taxes at a much higher rate.

With the hundreds of conventional funds available, how do you narrow down the choices? The "experts" have a ton of theories and calculations used to evaluate mutual funds. Here are my recommendations. My recommendations are of how to pick not which one(s) to pick. First, find one that is made up of the type of stocks you believe are good and profitable. Then review the past performance of the fund. Look up the amount (percentage) that it made on average per year for the last 10 years. If the fund has not been around for 10 years look at the last 5 years. If it has not been around that long you can look up the numbers labeled "*since inception*" which means since it started. Keep in mind that a fund that has been around for a long time is easier to evaluate than one without much of a history to look at. If you like the ones that are made of technical companies, there may not be that many that have been around for a long time.

One more thing that is real important about evaluating past history (performance) of a mutual fund. If you look at just the recent history of a fund, like for the last month or even the last quarter and it seems really good, you will be tempted to pick it. Understand that is the past history of the fund. Something may have caused the price of the fund to jump. The cost to invest in that fund may be higher than normal now and would limit how much of the fund you can invest in. So stick with one that has a long term history of good performance.

Oh yeah, for the record when you invest in a mutual fund you are actually buying shares in the fund. Shares, just like buying stock shares in a company. Think of the mutual fund as a company. In this case the "company" deals with stock and/or bonds, instead of a regular company that deals with widgets.

And, even though you are buying shares, some funds will call them "units", you actually are investing "dollars." You don't actually buy specific numbers of shares as in stocks. Another difference is that the value assigned to each share, or unit, is technically called the net asset value (NAV). The *Net Asset Value* is simply the total current value of all of the assets of the fund divided by the number of shares.

# Chapter Eighteen

## How to Invest in Mutual Funds

The next logical thing we need to deal with in regards to mutual funds is - how do you get into them? Investing in mutual funds is a bit more difficult than putting your money in a savings account or even buying United States Savings Bonds. However, like so many other things, computers have even made investing in mutual funds easier.

To be able to invest in mutual funds you will need to open an account with a company, or firm, that deals different mutual fund companies or runs their own funds. The company that I use is now very accessible online. However, when I began using them I had to use something called a "phone" and have an application "mailed" using a thing called an "envelope." I then had to "mail" it back using a "stamp." If you are not sure of what these things are go ask you parents, maybe even your grandparents. Now you can just apply online.

Once your account is established you then have to choose which mutual fund, or funds, you would like to have your money put into. By being able to have different individual mutual funds you can "divide up" your money. For example, you might want to have one fund to save money for retirement and another to save for college expenses.

When you are ready to pick a mutual fund company, remember the terms in the last chapter like "no-load" and "risk". Go online and search for mutual funds, you will find tons of them. Now I don't want to have you become discouraged so if you need a place to start try www.Janus.com, the Janus Company, for example has been around awhile. They have a number of funds to choose from. They even have some specialized types of investments which you can read about on their site.

A brand new type of mutual fund available is called an asset allocation target fund (also called a life-cycle fund). With an *asset allocation target fund* you pick the year in which you would like to begin withdrawing. The fund will automatically adjust the type of investments held within the fund over time. Initially the fund will mostly be made up of equities (stocks) and other volatile investments. As your target date approaches, the fund will shift to more conservative (less risky) investments such as bonds. This all has to do with TIME as discussed previously. Early losses that may have happened with the volatile portion will have had more that enough time to have been made up. Also remember that risky stocks will, at times, provide a better return (more value).

With asset allocation target funds you don't have to worry about changing your portfolio yourself as time goes by. A *portfolio* in this case means your investment. Just keep putting your money in and it will keep growing and growing and will be ready when you want to use it.

# Chapter Nineteen

## Dollar Cost Averaging

At this point you now know <u>HOW</u> to invest your money, <u>WHERE</u> to invest your money, and of course <u>WHY</u> to invest your money. As far as how much to save and invest - the answer is, **as much as possible**. But, of course, you want to spend some of your money, right? Don't get nervous, remember, back in the beginning, part of your saving and investing plan involved spending, so spend that.

The best way to invest in stocks or mutual finds is through a method referred to as dollar cost averaging. *Dollar cost averaging* is when you put the same amount of money into your investment each time over a period of time. For example, every month you move 50 dollars from your retirement container into your mutual fund (or to buy stocks). So what makes this special? When you do this you end up buying more shares of stock, or more shares/units of a mutual fund, when the price per share happens to be lower than higher. In the end you will always have bought more lower priced shares than higher priced ones.

The next page has a chart to show how this works

Take a gander (which means look) at this.

| Amount invested | Share price | Number of Shares |
|---|---|---|
| 100.00 | 10.00 | 10 |
| 100.00 | 20.00 | 5 |
| 100.00 | 5.00 | 20 |

So now using some basic math, let's talk about this example.  First you have bought 35 shares. And you have invested $300.00.  Your average price per share is about $ 8.60, which does not mean much in this example, I just wanted you to see that I know about averages.  Here is the important part; you have **30** shares costing $10.00 or less and <u>only</u> **5** shares costing you more than $10.00.  As the price per share goes up you automatically have more lower priced shares all set to make money!  And following along the same way, you have less shares that cost more to lose value if the price goes down.  This is another cool way to have your money work for you.  Another way that dollar cost averaging helps, is that it protects you from losses that could occur if the price per unit, or share, drops significantly right after you invest.

You have to decide how much and how frequently, the interval, to move your money. Remember the key here is to invest the same amount of money each time. It could be every month or every time one of your containers or account gets to a certain amount. If you are a using a bank account remember not to empty it. For example, every time you get to $100.00 move $50.00 into your mutual fund or funds.

Or how about this? Put all your money into your savings account and when it gets to a certain point, let's say 500.00 THEN divide up $400.00, $40.00 is your charity or giving money, $120.00 gets sent to your Retirement investment, $120.00 goes to your Savings investment,. And of course, you get to spend/use $120.00. This will leave $100.00 in your bank account which will keep your bank happy.

This way you will not have a bunch of money just sitting around your house.

This is how my son does it, except that he has his account set to automatically transfer set amounts of money each week from his bank account to other investments.

And of course, I have the same amount from my paycheck every two weeks go to my retirement investment. My saving and spending amount shifts back and forth somewhat, but that is allowed when you get older. The same amount goes to my church every Sunday and frequently I use some of my spending money for other charitable causes.

# Chapter Twenty

## Credit Cards

In today's world there is no way to become, and to stay, in good financial shape without understanding credit cards. In fact many knowledgeable people frequently refer to the "dangers of credit card debt" as one of the most significant problems facing America today.

Let's start with the origin of credit cards. Many years ago if you went into a store and did not have the money to pay for your stuff, the owner would pull out a book and write down the amount that you owed. When you sold a horse or harvested and sold your crops you would go back to the store and "pay your debt". Another way to pay your debt would be to give the proprietor (owner) something that he could sell, fresh eggs for example. In this case you would be paying off the credit that the owner of the store gave you so that you could get the things that you needed to live.

Frequently when people bought things on credit they were embarrassed that they did not have the money to pay for the things on the spot. People would work very hard to pay off this credit debt as soon as possible. This was a matter of pride because respectable people did not owe others money, at least for little things. About the only debt that was not considered embarrassing would be a loan, or mortgage, for land. People needed land to farm and live on. These mortgages were usually from banks and like the others were paid on schedule and on time. Store owners were very careful as to whom, and when, they would allow credit. This is because the money they were owed was money that they needed to buy more things for their store to sell <u>and</u> it was the money that they needed to pay the suppliers that provided the things that the people without money used. This was very important and the people granted credit understood it and appreciated the trust from those providing credit.

OK so how did we get to the credit cards of today? About 60 years ago a group of restaurant owners in New York City got together and decided to offer their very best, in this case richest, customers a new way to pay for their meals. They made up a little card that the diners, the people who ate at any of their restaurants, could present in any one of these eateries, and at the end of the month would receive a single bill. TA DAH, the birth of the credit card. The idea caught on and a company called MasterCard began issuing cards to the public as well as convincing merchants that this was a good thing and would help their sales. Around the same time large stores, Sears for example, replaced keeping track of store credit in a ledger with a their own store credit card. Back to MasterCard, MasterCard would give the merchants the money to pay for the things that the card was used to buy, and then would send a bill to the customers to pay the debt on the card. Back then you had to be in pretty good financial shape to have a credit card. You would have to have a job as well as a good relationship with a bank and have a fair amount of money, or stocks, sitting in a bank or brokerage firm.

As the economy grew and more people were working, more and more people "qualified" for a MasterCard. Eventually other general credit cards, as opposed to individual store credit cards, began to appear. Why did this happen? Easy, to make money!! How? Some credit card companies charge a set amount to have the cards and the holder of the card would have to pay the entire amount on the card every month. Others would let you pay back the amount over time and charge you interest on the money owed on the card. Just like banks charge money, interest, on the money that you borrow from a bank.

In fact it became a matter of prestige, being special, to even have a card. Remember, originally only the best qualified, financially secure, people had credit cards because the companies that issued them wanted to make sure that they got their money back, and then some. As more and more people got cards, they lost the prestige associated with having them. So what did the credit card companies do to put it back in? They made some of the cards special. When I was your age credit cards had become fairly common for adults. I remember the first time that I saw a "gold" MasterCard. Boy was I impressed. Eventually more and more people had the gold version. Guess what happened next? You got it, another special card was created, this time "platinum". As of this writing "titanium" is the special card. But you know what? I do not believe that any of the cards have any "prestige" any more. There are just so many out there and anybody can get them. So just like with "widgets" there are so many out there – who cares. Supply outweighs demand. The "care" should be the problems caused by credit cards, not "who has one".

In case you are wondering why I am spending so much time on credit cards with you, there is a reason. In today's society *credit card debt* is a HUGE problem. **Credit card debt** by the way is the amount of money that you owe the credit card companies after using the card(s) to buy things. Why is it a problem? Easy. Most people do not pay off the debt right away. In fact, many have such a large amount, or balance, that they do not earn enough money to ever pay it off!  The credit companies charge interest on the money that you owe, the more money you owe, the more interest is charged.  AND it works against you in the same way that compound interest helps you in a savings account.  That is that you are being charged, or accumulating, interest on the interest that you already have been charged.

Speaking of interest, the amount of interest that credit companies charge is usually very high.  In fact it is so high that if you went to a bank for a loan and they wanted to charge you the same interest rate you would never agree to the loan because of the interest rate.  So why are people willing to pay that much to credit card companies?  Because now-a-days most people are financially dumb.  Why do you need to know this, because it is, and always has been, my goal to make you financially smart.

When you have a balance on your credit card, the company tells you how much the minimum amount you have to pay each month.  If you pay the minimum only, and put nothing more on your card it could take many years to pay it off and would end up costing you hundreds, if not thousands of dollars in interest.  Oh yeah, if your late with the minimum payment, they will charge you late fees and some will even use it as excuse to raise the interest rate you are being charged.

Take a look at this credit card situation.

| Balance ($) | Rate | Payment ($) | Paid off |
|---|---|---|---|
| 5000.00 | 15% | 100.00 | 87 months |
| 10,000.00 | 17% | 200.00 | 88 months |
| 20,000.00 | 17% | 300.00 | 204 months |

This is an illustration of how long it would take you to pay off your credit card debt.  By the way, 204 months is 17 Years !!!  And are you ready for this, you will have paid almost $ 42,000 in interest.

So what makes this whole credit thing different than the beginning of credit at the general store 100 years ago, or even the original "Diners Club" card? What makes this debt different than reasonably acceptable debt such as mortgages for houses and land?   The old general store issued credit for necessities for living and/or survival.  Not for things like *Playstations,* televisions, or DVDs, or MP3 players. People took pride in what they earned and had.  People respected those who provided credit and would pay off the debt in a timely fashion.

Why is it important that you understand this? I will say it again – <u>You Cannot Be in Good Financial Shape if you have a bunch of credit card debt</u>.

Now that you understand the problems with carrying **C**redit **C**ard **D**ebt, what can you do about it?

# Don't Get into CCD

Some of you might be thinking – "why are you telling me this, I'm just a kid". Simple, because very soon you will be getting credit card offers in the mail. I am sure that you already have seen many on the internet. Your parents get offers all of the time. It used to be that only the people that could pay the debt would receive offers. Not any more. People without any money or those who owe tons of money can get cards. People without jobs get offered cards. You would not believe the offers my wife gets, and she has not had a job in many years. In other words she has no income but companies are willing to give her

$25,000 – that is twenty-five thousand dollars – credit to spend.

(I am shouting now) SHE HAS NO PERSONAL INCOME TO PAY OFF THE DEBT SHE CAN PUT ON THE CARD (if she accepted it).  How crazy is that?

Hopefully you're thinking – "I don't want this to happen to me, I will never get a credit card".  But, are you ready for this?  It is OK to have ONE credit card AND always pay it off every month in full.  Only use it for things that you can afford to pay off right away.  In other words you should only put on it amounts that you have in your "spending" account, or if it is something more expensive (but also important) you then can use your "savings" funds.  And there may be times when an "emergency" happens.  Maybe you are on a trip and you break your eyeglasses, or somebody steals your suitcase with all of your clothes.  How about this one, you're on a trip with some friends and they start doing things that you know are bad, dangerous, or even against the law, and you needed to leave and go home right away, another good use for a credit card.

There is something else that works much like a credit card without the potential problems. It is called a "debit card". A *Debit Card* looks like a credit card, and even works like a credit card to pay for things. However, when you use a **Debit Card** the money comes right out of your bank account to make the payment. You never build a balance that has to be paid off. This way you do not get into CCD trouble.

Another option that works well if you are going on a trip is something called a pre-paid credit card, which actually works more like a debit card. With *a pre-paid credit card* money is actually "put into the card" account through the issuing company before you can use it. For example, your parents get you a card because you are going on a band trip and they do not want you carrying cash. You then put in $100.00 from your "spending" account. You are now able to buy things with your card as long as they do not add up to more than $100.00. When you get back if you want to put more money into it you can. Keep in mind that the issuing company is around to make money themselves. Some charge a certain amount when you put money in. Meaning you might put in $100.00 but you only have $95.00 to spend, they get to keep $5.00. Some charge you every month that you have the card, meaning that they take some of your money in the card away.  And some even do both.

This is why our 16 year old son now carries a bank debit card instead of the pre-paid card that he took to Spain with his Spanish Club.  In fact, although it truly is a debit card, meaning it works like a debit card, it is accepted anyplace that accepts MasterCard credit cards, which is almost everywhere.  In other words, he can use it like a credit card, BUT, the money immediately comes out of his bank account.

# Chapter Twenty-One

## The Summary

In the beginning we talked about the origins and uses of money. It was actually fairly simple in those times. A common mutually acceptable means was created to obtain certain "necessities". Notice I used the word necessities. People back then, for the most part, only needed necessities. Only needing and working to get the things used to live made things a whole lot simpler.

For some reason our culture, and of course the media, are real good at making us believe that we "need" all kinds of things. It is very easy to get sucked into this way of thinking. Half of the problem occurs when we want or get things that we cannot afford. Society makes us feel that we cannot be happy unless we have everything we want or things that society says we need. And to make things worse, once we have some of these things, we are pushed into believing that we "need" even more. If you ever have a chance to spend any time at all in a third world village – take it. This will show you that you can be happy without a ton of stuff. The other half occurs when we purchase things that we cannot afford. This most often happens now-a-days when people are not very, very careful when using a credit card.

You must start saving, and managing your money starting right now. We discussed an easy way to manage and save your money – do it now. The next step was to invest it. You have to put your money to work.

Money just sitting around loses it's *buying power*. This means that because as time passes things will cost more. In other words, the ten dollars sitting in your drawer today will not buy the same ten dollars worth of stuff in twenty years. By investing your money wisely, it should not only retain its buying power, but also increase in value to be worth even more as time goes on.

# Chapter Twenty-Two

## The Conclusion

OK guys, we are almost finished. In this not so big of a book, we have covered some of the most important things that you will need to survive in today's world. Understanding money and how it works is an absolute necessity. To continue growing towards being happy and content, you have to have a good handle on this entire "money thing". You always need to be in control of your money and the way you spend your money.

Understanding the ways to "put your money to work" now, while you are still young, is a HUGE advantage when it comes to investing.  So go ahead and get started right away.

Don't forget to be a charitable and a good all around person.  There are many "worthy" charitable organizations out there that could use your help, either with your "giving" money or your time.  As a matter of fact, getting into the college of your choice, or getting the job you really want could have a lot to do with the volunteer, charity, or mission work that you have done.

## Take Care !!